I dedicate this to my beautiful wife Vicky, and my wonderful family. A massive thank you to Oliver Brierley for his wonderful illustrations.

I hope this book gives a platform for Dementia.

Front Cover Attribution

Contents

Parts of me

I'm awake with the first steps of the
day, I head towards the toilet but I'm
feeling an empty shell a "husk".

I make my way to the kettle for the
daily routine of a coffee but forgot to
switch it on.

Oh well! not to worry it's just a hiccup,
I'm on my way to my destination of my
seat for the day.

Check me out I didn't forget that one.

I'm comfy now remote in hand, coffee
in the other, oh what important
decisions I can make alone..

Day's lead into a steady reel of
continuation, there's no gaps in
between.

"Oh, don't forget your medication"
shouts a voice, of course I won't it's my
highlight of the day..

It feels like someone has took my soul,
thrown it down a dark pit, and I'm
trying to catch up with it, to keep hold
of being ME.

I know slowly people walk in and out,
but love travels in a different path, it's
more grounded, it leaves deeper
footprints.

I hope to capture images and sentiments
to take them into my small world.

Identity is everything but more
importantly I'm on a "journey", it may
deviate, it may swerve a lot soon, but
memories I'm taking" them" with me…

I take snippets and samples, also pieces
in my memory, these are for the journey

ahead, I'm hoping you're in there with
me, to stabilise my balance..

I'm sure on my journey, or hope I have,
left some kind of imprint on someone
somewhere.

Make memories not stories.

Make impressions not shadows.

Share not indulge, but more importantly
show love whenever and wherever...

My journey is exactly that, mine, but
yours will hopefully be longer,
healthier, wiser, and crammed packed
with memories......

SENDING love to MY Loved ones.

Days all in One

There are no set days in a week, just a
continuation of days merging into each
one.

A stumble or fall is soon forgotten not
even a memory of it, the surroundings
become somewhat blurred but there's
always something that is sharp and
focused, and it seems to keep me
looking at it; such a strange feeling.

Orientation is definitely a "thing" in my
world, you get up, move, step, or walk
and the world is faster than you; such a
weird feeling.

I'm told daily I'm doing good
"considering", but what does that even
mean? I'm a person but not, I'm me but
"am I"?

I search but don't find, I travel but only
in mind.

The path is narrow, but wider in parts,
but not wide enough.

Always wanting more, never enough,
keep on walking without moving.

Life's tough, but good, my reflection is
blurred, but to me, it's crystal clear.

D, for determination

E, for effort

M, for motivation

E, for emotions

N, for new

T, for time

I, for imagination

A, for all

See I can't even finish my daily journal
without spelling dementia I needed
spell-check. My love to those who
deserve it....

A Journal Contains

My weekly journal.

I felt/feel like I've shed a layer of me,
left it somehow behind, either not
needed or wanted.

Definitely feeling more and more
isolated, seem to snap so easily, but
"that's not me".

Not all changes are good ones, I'm
trying to adapt to this new life, but the
path is wide.

I know my struggles are not alone, but
how far am I casting my shadow?

I wish to progress forward, but in one
piece, not segmented, aims and
aspirations are high but not, and
inspirations are low..

My footprints are getting shallow, but
I'm treading deep??

I have moments of internal isolation but
moments of congestion, sometimes
together..

Places become adventures, that become
imagination, all in a blink. What started
as a "good thing" becomes a "why"?

Seeing seems enviable but blindness
feels real, I see now what you don't, but
is that good or bad, or another
adventure..

Understanding now is good for "ME",
but judgement comes with a price, I'm
sure I've paid my price twice over.

If my journey can be shared or
comforted then I'm not alone, and a
journey I'm willing to share.

A Movement In.

Time is relevant and passes by, but my
time feels irrelevant and timeless at the
same moment.

I am not seeing movements of time, but
"captions", that I need to put into place.
I'm having a roller-coaster without the
"fun", but I'm still me, smiling and
happy.

Slowing down in reactions but
travelling too fast to appreciate. I'm still
the same as ever, just wrapped
differently, just a few extra layers.

Study the person not the persona, judge
less and you will see more, that's when
you're see me, properly.

Laughter is meditation, but nurturing is
medicine, leave an impression not
depression and talk do not grin.

I'm alive as ever, just wearing different
kind of glasses, but I see very clearly

"thank you", I just responded
differently.
Remember my actions and cherish the
reactions, as I leave you with only a
"splash" of what you deserve in my
return!

A Blind Vision

When you pull your blinds, it's to see
clearer, especially whilst it's sunny, but
my blinds are set on "auto".

My mind is the remote and this allows
my mind to "close the light of life", in
an instant, to allow a clear vision.

Whilst you are living, I am to, you are
within a structure, I'm within a
construction, you have limitations I
have imagination.

Cast your net and see what you catch, I
will too, alongside yours, you can be
my guide, and I'll be your strength, you
can be my comfort whilst "I'll be there
too".

If "I come back", it's because of you, if
"I stay a while", it's because of me.

You can start and I'll follow, as where
your footprints are, there you will find
my shadow.

If I choose to follow, then feel the
"love", don't just sense it. I'm on my

path, guided by "good intensions",
remember, I allow you to be here
alongside me, but only in part, this is
my passage, so I journey alone, parts of
the way.

I "cherish" moments, I can steal
emotions, I can capture reality, but I can
also take heart.

Whilst I can, I shall, when I can't, I will
imagine and when it's possible to, I will
remember.

Family is your foundation, so make it
strong..
We all come in alone, and will go out
alone, but make sure, in between, enjoy
"the love"..

Steps Away.

When someone says, step aside, step
up, or even step down, you will make a
"slight" movement.
But my next "step" will be more of a
hop or leap into my "new world".

This world, I will only be visiting from
time to time, I have been invited to
visit, not to stay, to see if I'm worthy.

Movement and momentum are not
measured here but processed and
observed and here I'm being processed
for acceptance.

I've promised I'll make no ripples or
waves, but I will help paint the
background.

I'm being "selected" for my next
destination, so I'm only in its departure
lounge, awaiting, but I am sure the wait
will be full of promise, and the journey,
fruitful, and my seat comfortable.

My luggage is light and is packed
accordingly, my clothes are bright and

colourful, to allow me to lead the way,
rather than depart, without a trace.

I've accepted my offer of a one way
ticket, because the return is open ended.

Whilst here on this "final destination", I
will send your thoughts and words to
loved ones, I'll share your memories
with them, but I'll want to keep their
reactions to cheer me on, for comfort
and acceptance.

Whilst I hope to leave a deep footprint,
it will I know gently fade away in time,
but the cast I set, and place will
hopefully sustain an impression.

Can I still Travel?

Sands of time" pass through
"restricted", but push through
effortlessly, enviably.

The first grain or even the last particle
do not complete the conclusion, until all
come together.

Same with my life, I will journey
through, with restrictions and
limitations and can only end this
journey, once all pieces are all together
again.

Though I travelled here alone, I've
travelled with abundance, passed
through fast, but observed in depth.

Time is my keeper, but its batteries are
my strength, by having quality ones, has
enriched my presence, and have been
used wisely.

We are all "time travellers", but we do
not realise it's meaning or structure, but
time allows us to have "pauses", that

allows reflection, regrets, and
management, it's how we use these
helpful "pauses" that define us.

I've had pauses and squandered them,
regrets I have had a few, but time
travels forward into possibilities, and
you do with it will underline your
definition of existence.

Dementia is cruel but can also be
reflective.

Dementia is scary, but also
adventurous. It's destructive but
constructive.

It's a positive reaction and not a
negative retraction.

So, in this my glass is most definitely
half "full" and not "empty".
I'll use this hurdle to explore and jump
over, and will not fall, I may allow
myself to stumble, knowing that my
"love one's" will surely support me.

I am trying to adapt, same as you are,
together we may not win the "battle",

but we surely will and can win the
"war".
Cast a wide net and not a shadow. Cast
a light not a cloud, I've CAST my
shadow as "far" as I dared, but not too
far as to spoil my "heaven"..

What am I?

I close my eyes and see a "husk an
empty shell", that's me, I'm shouting,
when did I become so empty.

My shell is cracked and fragile, but the
nut is hard, I'm seeing life images in
forms of "frozen" moments, paused for
my deliberation.

Why, I don't know, is it to evaluate or
deliberate? not sure.

Is time asking me to "judge" or "justify"
my life and its footprint, or just another
"captive" emotion in this quiet, lonely
spot.

I try to open the shell, and "shout", the
old Happy go-lucky Andy is here, but
my captive demon holds on to me
laughing.

I may have restrictions or life restraints,
but inside I'm bursting with joy and
"let's party", like I'm trying to say "hi,
I'm here"...

I want so much, to allow my memory to be my shell, and allow it not to hollow out and wither away, but leave or blow away in strength and comfort, before any of my "cherished" loved ones see a miserable old shallow shell or a husk of the person I was and want to be again ...

Here Together

Close your eyes, relax, empty your
mind, feel the tranquillity, then I'm
ready to hold your hand, and slowly
walk with you and allow you to see and
feel my "special" place of magic.

Here please observe and listen, what
you feel is a cloud coming towards us to
enclose us, it's a glow that's created
from love and care, that smells of candy
floss, flowers, cotton linen, it's blessed
and shared and "found" us, to make you
and I "welcome", so stay with me eyes
closed, but mind open, and you witness
this place of magic, that's our "comfort
zone", can you feel it.

You can sense, you can see and hear,
but what's really happening is your
mind has been opened by a thought
direction, a gift, given to only persons
deserving of this magical visitation.

It's a place of contemplation,
imagination, but a special safe place,
given by loved and cherished, good
people.

In this "loaned" capsule of time, enjoy being with me here, feel the love ruminating all around, its direction is at this time comforted by your presence, and I "thank you" for coming with me here today, but only take back what you need, in our minds we've shared just in a moment.

You may open your eyes now, knowing I'm with you in both worlds and always will be...

Where to Go?

A path is created, designed, to allow
passage and travel along its route, to
simplify the effort and safely get you to
its end.

It can be a lonely one, or an exciting
one, it can be mysterious or even
unexpected, but where the path takes
you to, is never assured, as it is or may
have unexpected imperfections,
deviations along its route.

A path can lead to greatness,
imaginative possibilities and at the
same time led to the complete opposite.

But you and I have a choice in its
destination, its outcome, and its
intension, we choose it's "end game".

Whether we choose good or bad in its
direction or it's impression.

I've made my path of life, created it and
designed it, by me, it's definitely not
perfect, but different, it has
imperfections, but it has good
foundations, I've made it strong, but

only strong enough for "my" loved
one's to step along its passage, to enjoy
the uncertainty of its destination.

I hope I've left and installed, a good
thoughtful, enjoyable path of
imagination, love, and kindness, that
helps light the way along your "path of
life", in wherever it takes or guides you,
in all its glory and fruitfulness.

A Box of Tricks

The lights are on but no one's in, I hear
music, but the house is empty, shh, do
you hear that, no I don't, I did.

The mind plays tricks, are you good
with magic, or just a spectator.
The mind is complex, has never been
re-created, people have tried but to no
avail.

When I leave, I'll blast up so fast in a
ball of light right up to the stars, there
I'll scatter stardust, to shine a light, just
for you.

I'll be there to brighten your way but not
too bright to slow you down, I'm the
hand that catches you, when you fall,
and I'll shelter you when it rains.

Your glow is so bright and stands alone,
it's a guiding show to where I'll go.

I'm never alone whilst you are here in
my heart, I'll cherish your prayers, I
store them in my memories, and read
when I'm all alone.

In this place of peace and love, is where
our loved one's dwell, there I will share
my lonely thoughts, and tell the stories
of our true love.

Even when I'm in that place, I'm never
alone when I have you.

You are my rock and my comfort too,
and will always be, "my true love"!

A Look in Hope

I'm looking through this pane of glass,
here they are, just passing by, and again
just passing through, where they go I
don't know, where they've been, I just
don't know, but all I know it's passed
me by, I'm still standing here, just
looking through.

They go so fast, they will travel far, or
travel wide, but not too long.

I'm still here looking through this pane
of glass.

My travels are still ahead, again not too
far, just out of reach, but not too far for
you to see.

Passing by, don't even speak, what are
we, trick or treat, or am I just a lullaby.
I'm here looking through this pane of
glass today, wiping away my pain of
heart, that's yearning for another day.

Here I am looking through this pane of
glass, waving through my breaking
heart, stop and look back, through this

pane of glass, and there I'll be looking
back, just to give a loving smile!!

Looking Glass

Here I am again, looking through this
pane of glass, why so vain, or is that
pain, whilst I look through this pane of
glass, then I realise it's my reflection
from this glass.

They travel so fast, passing by, they
don't even see or listen, but then it
stops, all a sudden, I can listen, I hear
their thoughts, and their sorrows, it's a
shame they don't hear me hollow , to
say, maybe it's tomorrow I share your
toils and troubles.

Reflections through this pane of glass,
helps me through my days of woe.
Everything's moving now, so fast and
loud, and I'm back looking through to
see you all.

Step back aside, and you're see, there
will always be side by side, you and me.

I'm still looking for your smile, that
glance, that ever looking chance, and
whilst I await, please look back and
glint with me in your eyes.

I wait for a chance just to hear those
words again, "that I love you".

On reflection through this glass I see,
what I need, I hear so clear, my need is
more, but rest assured, it's not enough,
I'll always need a little more.

I'm going now, I'll be here again,
looking for your ever smile, I come here
often, so should you, to see me through
these thoughts of mine.

You're welcome back anytime, but don't
be surprised if I don't remember, our
last time, as this can be our first time.

I'm living with this disease, and it lives
here within, but never will I lose this
fight, I'll bite and fall and battle
through, all the time I'm here with you.

Carry me through, our darkest times,
and I promise you, I'll enlighten you!!!

Call Me

Here I am sitting by the telephone,
waiting for you to call, to hear all about
your day today. I'll sit and wait still
some more, until I hear your voice some
more, and talk all about your day.

There it goes, my telephone, ringing me
and letting me know you're there once
more, I hear you moan about today and
then some more, but still, I hear you
groan some more, all about you once
again.

I'm sitting here all alone, by my
telephone, I hear so much, I say no
words, yet still you moan, I feel your
soul, and your words, so continue to tell
too much and I'm here to say it's all OK.

I want to hear you say, how's your day,
but that's for another day, so while I
wait for your words, to be repaid, I'll sit
and wait another day.

Your voice to me is worth the wait, so I
sit and pause until I hear that voice
some more, all I hear is why the wait,
but you definitely are worth the wait.

Please tell me more, continue on, I'd
love to hear, why this is, I don't know,
that's for another day.

Then you call to hear my voice, you
want to hear some more, about my day,
but that can't be another day, for my day
has gone away from here to another
place.

Where now I sit is alone, on my own by
this phone, I'd wished you had rung,
about my day all alone, by this phone,
now I'm gone away from here, I'm not
alone by my phone, I'm just on my
other line calling home, about being
alone.

I hear so much, but not enough, whilst
here alone, I say too much, yet not
enough, for you to listen, I'm here
today, but not tomorrow, as oh, by the
way, you're far too late, I've gone away
to this place, all alone, there's a
fireplace, I will sit and wait again once
more, because it's all about your day
once more.

Keep coming back for more, each and
every day, and I'll try and listen more
and more all about your day just some
more.

I want you today and tomorrow more
and more, be true and be sure, share
your troubles less, understand more, it's
not about knowing more, but learning
all so much more about what's real, so
keep yourself here today, just for now,
alone and listen, then you're know
you're not all alone.

As I'm here too, with you now, together
with shall sit by this phone, just to hear
it ring just once more.

By my phone here I will say that you
have a voice, but listen too, and then
you will know why you sit here, just
like me, by your phone.

There is another way communicate so
listen and I'll speak to you in a way for
you to hear, about our day.

Thoughts of

Food for thought, or thoughts of food, I
know which one is for me.

Sweets, cakes and so much more, there
for me to enjoy, I thought I heard you
say, do you want more, but that's just
me.

My pleasures are but a few, so I'll
endure this all alone, and adjust this pile
of stuff.

My happiness is my retreat, in this place
is a rare repeat, of for where I am, here
is now, my time is safe and stored for
now.

In these times with my treats, I am free
to choose, and design their fate.

My choices are now but a few and my
sweets are my retreat.

In these repeats of words and of sweets,
are what I am, I'm just a man on my
way, so just repeat with me, it's all OK.

I'm here today and while I stay, I'll
repeat and say, it's me today.

I'm on a loop, today, but tomorrow is
another day, so while we're here enjoy
my sweets, they're here with me.

But ask tomorrow, I might say, because
it's all a game, here you say, I may
repeat what you say, but sweets are ours
to gain and obtain, so enjoy and contain
the love we've shared with my sweets,
here today.

Reflection of

The great *Louis Armstrong* said, "trees are green, red Roses too, I've seen them bloom from me to you, and I say to myself, what a wonderful world"

and whilst I am in my world of calm, my green is brighter, the red, so more radiant, the bloom is amazing, it's most definitely a wonderful world.

BUT I arrive back from here, to your smile, your beautiful eyes, and that ever glowing shine and it reminds me, this worlds not so bad.

My captions and relapses are only reminders for ME, to ensure that you, and only you, are my guide, my light, showing me how blessed I am..

Whilst I "mind travel", and adventure away, your inspiration allows my return trip, to be easily led, through the emotions in the way.

Strength I take, guidance I steal and emotion I keep, are "things" that come from" you to me ", I need these

strengths to hold me through, these
awful days, they guide away the
thoughts of strive.

Only in your shadow am I ever safe, so
please, keep me close, cast your shadow
and there, I'll stay, safe and warm for
another day.

You are an angel of that I'm sure, here,
and now and that's for sure, that keeps
me pure and cured, again for sure.

On my worse days, you hold my hand,
the good days we share more, the my
"lows" are poor but, my highs are pure
with you for sure.

Please keep your prayers and thoughts,
not for me, but for this Angel, who is as
pure, and sure, and keeps her heart for
me in every way.

I'll never be able to say enough, each
and every day, how much you are my
guiding star"!!

Sands of Time

Sands of time, or time in hand.
Up or down, right, or wrong.

Are these just weird or different ends?

What is real, and what is a dream, am I
awake or is my dream a reality?

As whilst I dream, I feel so alive, but
while I'm awake I feel, not quite here, I
feel different, but when I'm there I'm
real, I'm part of, I'm accepted, I'm me
again.

In this existence, I'm just a part of here,
a part not, I am calm, but it's not. I'm
bursting yet deflated all within this
captivity.

My allocation is limited, my ability, not
quite right, but I imagine so well, so
inside I design, outside I just appear,
my vision is clear, yet is it really clear
here.

Confusion and me, are joined in part,
but friends we're not, but find our paths
are inter twinned, going somewhere, in

vain or gain, being apart is not our end
game.

So here and now, or there and why,
whatever is if, and so can I be, all alone,
or be re-framed.

I wish I could, but sometimes not, so
today I'll stay, but yesterday no.

I'll return again into this time, this
place, to re-adjust my mind, to re-align
my body into this world, to replace
what was, to what is.

If I come back to where is now, all I
know is that's the plan, to be here right
now, to reschedule , I will escape
sometimes, but capture in this thought, I
am, I will, I shall, I can, I have and I do,
so at all times spare this thought with
you today..

Selfish

When did I become such a "git", who
has an acid tongue, and definitely no
filter?

I see clear situations, but answer,
blindly, I hear so well, but deaf to what
I'm not prepared to hear.

But my reactions are quick as ever,
insults come easy, and yet, delayed and
can be different, when it chooses to.

I'm bloody sure, this disease chose me
for a reason, testing me, what for, not
sure, but I will find out.

I'm still here inside, and yet seem not to
be, life's decisions and opportunities
seem not to be mine, but selected,
everyone has selected their opinions,
sieved through, and given their
outcome, even before I've even blinked.

I HAVE Dementia, but, it does not
HAVE me, please remember that.

My moments of "pauses", allow
reflection of importance.

My tremors "allow" me to re-adjust to here and now.

Once I'm realigned, and paused to go again, remember, I will be fresh, renewed and myself again, so I'm still ME, but maybe, just maybe, you too should, "pause", to re-adjust, allow yourself to re-align, then you may just, and I say may adjust, your judgement, your vision and, definitely, you will see and hear more clearly.

I'm aware of, I'm tuned in to, I'm alert too, but I'm also NOT, just depending on the day, so before making quick decisions, check to see what "day it is"...

Oh, and by the way, it's, Tuesday...... "I think"...

Mind Travel

You can, but I won't.

I can't, but you did.

What if, but not now.

Why not, but it could be.

All reasons of, but not reasonable to me.

Selections of mind, but mindful of collection.

I can manipulate, but not stipulate.

Most definitely, but not sure enough.

I travel, but yet, I'm still here.

My mind allows all of these to contemplate my fate, but yet, not answer the one question relevant.??

In this mind of mine, or mind of ours, we strive and achieve, but do we know, that our spirit is" free" to deliver the answer we require, which is??

Am I enough??

Am I enough, enough am I, I am
enough, all the same, but vastly
different, just shows how little we
know, but yet, we feel we know
enough, to make judgement, opinions,
on others, or each of us, without seeing
and looking inwardly?

I know I am; I know I can, and I know I
will, can you say the same.

Time yourself out, reflect, digest, and
contemplate, and only then will, you
and I see clearly, into our shared
"solace".

So, remember, re-connect, embrace, and
together our next steps will be
"collective".

In these words, and feelings, find me,
search for me, help me, and you will be
rewarded in this abundance.

Our heart is our vision, our sight be our
enlightenment, and hearing can be our
filter to our dreams, our life and hopes.

I share a moment, a particle of "your" time, but I "give" you, an eternal embrace, to capsulate and comfort you, through all of "your" journeys.

Time in Hand

I see the clock, I hear it tick, it seems so
loud, tick tock, tick tock.

Forward it goes, never to stop, not even
for me.

A second, a minute even an hour, is it
morning, afternoon, or evening, or is
this just a moment.

It's night and day, it's all the same
ticking away.

Where am I, within this time, or this
puzzle of time.

Am I an Edge, a middle or a centre
piece, or could I be your missing piece?

Do I complete this picture of time, or
just become another piece?

The clock is ticking so loud, I want to
reflect upon its movement, but it ticks
alone, with no control.

Where is this time of here and now, this
time of ours, we're find our place, our
time to taste?

Why this time of here and now, this
time of ours, it's ticking loud, so I'm
awake in this moment in time, to see
why, it's choice of here and now.

Time allows reflection, it's here, and
there, plenty of it, for us to share, but
still, there's much more for those to
share.

Take time, share time, and enjoy your
time and "laugh" with time, only then
can time be your friend.

I've used my time, I had my time, and
with thought and process, and yet,
sometimes not, it's too short, but yours
is not, so don't stare at my clock, look at
yours, and then, you will know, time is
not slow.

It's not even fast, it's going forward,
onwards, to guide you, allow you time.
Time to love, to share, to cherish and
enjoy, as it's only, "passing through"..

Confusing

Can you see time, can you hear that
vision, can you smell that sound or even
touch the music?

All mixed up, bandaged, all confused,
in the waiting room, to be re-arranged,
putting back in place.

In life, I repaired, I replaced and even
returned, all into its place, completed,
sorted, to be re-purposed.

I've bandaged, I've wrapped, I've even
sprayed, to regain its use once again.

But confusion is just a combination of
mixed imaginations, that need
assembling, to re-purposes its
usefulness.

I need arranging, at times, needing
bandaging, only sometimes, and fixing
often.

So, whilst I await my turn, my
appointment to "be seen", and assessed,

I'll read a book and observe, to focus
on, away from my pain, as I need
repairing, I often do.

In my repairs, my mixed up parts,
they're being put back together to where
I'm not too sure, but in their place.

My bandages are off, I'm not mixed up
now, I "see" the vision, I "hear" the
sound, and "smell" so well.

So, whilst I'm "good to go", let's mix
this sound, move around, party on and
gather around.

I once did repair, but not no more, I was
replaced and left unlaced, it's not the
same anymore, but I still want some
more, oh so much more.

My bandages are all cut away, scars are
healed, but my memories are faded, I'm
a distant thought, I "was" here, to
repair, but sadly not no more..

Symbolic or Simplistic

I'm here by myself, listen I hear a
sound, but no-one's around.

So, I'll sit and listen to my thoughts and
prayers, and whilst I do, I'll share with
you, a thought or two.

In these thoughts that I have of you, I
seem to see, that it's hard for you, so I
pray some more, and whilst I do, my
eye's fill up, with tears and sorrow, as
there will be no more tomorrows.

My minds expressed these tears of love,
to reassure my heart, that whilst I travel
away some days, but not too far, that
my love stays with me all of these days.

I look upon my wedding ring, it's
symbolic meaningful thought and on its
continuing loop, reminding me of my
love for you.

Remove the ring now I'm gone, and
there you're see, my ring's still on, as
my body's engraved itself, to ensure my
love of you and it will never fade away.

So here again, all alone, deep in thought
about you and me, as now I see I'm not
alone, even now you're with me in truth.

Heart and soul we muster through, so
I'll take with me today, and tomorrow,
if that's OK, all that's pure and true, and
I'll keep it warm and safe for my "rainy
days"..

Dementia or Demented

You decide, I decide, don't us bother, as
it has chosen its side.

Did I digest this disease, inhale it,
breath it, absorb or even step in it,
because if so, the cheeky "sod" slipped
past me, without a sign, just slipped on
through, just to hide and grow, here
inside.

It plays its game, of hide and seek, it
plays a game every day, just to see, if

I'm here for it to wind me up.
As it passes through and it travels out, it
has its grip and it has a cold frosty
touch, but whilst I maybe warm outside
it's in here, in me , just to show it's just
got some more pieces of me.

Why choose me, or challenge me, and
why now, is this a game, to play with
me, to hold on tight, so it's on its path,
playing tricks, it's kicking me, hitting
out, and smiling, whilst I'm in this pain
of mine.

I feel it has its plan, of this I'm pretty
sure, within its plan it has for me, so I
will go along and play this game just a
little more, just so I can gain the upper
hand and then we're see if it's playing a
game of "hide and seek".

So, whilst Dementia plays out it's game
with me today, I'll sit here and study it
more,, I'll observe its game of mind
control, as then I can challenge back
and play along with its game, so then
I'll have the "upper hand".

I will fight along with it some more
today and with this I'm sure, I will
tomorrow a little more, so as whilst I
do, I'll challenge you to play along with
me, this long lasting game of "party
tricks", and as we do, play along
together, we're confuse this disease of
mine, to show it's awful hand, to
weaken it's hold, and whilst it does, I'll
hold your hand, and together we will
win this fight, this game of "mind
control"..

Reflect or Reflection

Whilst I'm on this "side", I'll reflect, so
maybe then, I'll just be this reflection of
myself inside.

I'll judge my life, I'll reflect on it's
worth, then again in reflection, on that
side, I'll see my worth upon this life.

My mirror is large and clear to see, its
reflection is what I see, but I'd rather
not, so I'll just reflect, a little more, to
see what you see "in" me.

It shows to me, in this reflection, an
open door to step on through, to see
what's there, but is this a door, or just an
opening for me once more.

But I'll step ahead into this door, to see
what's there for me, and whilst I do,
please continue to look for me, as I'm
only in there to see what's there, I'm not
wanting to stay, as you're not there, but
my mind, loves to explore, so I'll tag
along, again some more, but not too
long.

I'll leave a little piece here for you, in
this place, so you're know where I am,
I'm in "that" place, just for now.

Pull the cord, pull it tight, hold it strong,
and pull me back, so I'll not stay away
in "that" place, away from you for too
long.

As I need you pulling me through on
these reflective days, showing me that
this dark place is not for me.

So, reflect this, and in reflection it
shows to me today, right now, that pull
on me, the stronger I become, but leave
it slack, I may slip away from here too
much.

So, I'll "shout" and "say" that, my
reflection is for me to reflect that
believe it or not
"I'm just a man"...

That Time Again

I'm here alone at 4am, wondering why I
can't sleep, then I sit and stare, I see
"that" world, the other side, wanting
me, calling me.

But today it's different as there's no
door to walk on through, it's just a
frame, but wider now, then I feel the
pull, it's pulling me through this frame,
now I'm through, to the "other" side.

I'm not sure why, but is it me, or am I
now different, as if it feels not quite
right.

But I'll walk along, just some more, to
see what I see, just to settle my own
curiosity.

It's different somehow, there are no
tree's, oh, and no people, or even
friends, to guide me on.

So, I'll walk until I see and feel the
warmth and glow I normally do, but
here today, it's strange that there's no
laughter and it's all silent and "not quite
right".

Then I see way ahead, in the distance,
movement, I hear noises, and I even
hear some music, so I walk some more,
that's when I see, that it's a party, it's
been arranged, for my delight, everyone
has gathered, they've all given me a
surprise, as it's all for me.

Now I'm alive once more, I'll stay here
for now, longer this time, I'll meet and
greet, and see what this takes from me,
or what is on offer for me.

It's been a blast, this party of mine,
we've had some fun, and dancing too,
but now I'll walk alone, back into "our"
world, with you waiting outside, for my
return.

I'll look back, just once more, to see my
family waving back at me, I wave back
too, saying "I love you", until we meet
again.

I'll shout out, I'll shout aloud, I'll say
those words again that "I love you", as

I'm shouting proud, it feels so good, I'm proud of all of you, my wonderful family.

But now I'm back, to this place, am I inside or outside, not quite sure about where I am, so am I home or am I still "there".

So, whilst I adjust my mind, please refrain your mind too, as I'm still me, just a little different each time.

I'm adjusting to this new timeline, to fit back in, so once I have, then you'll see a "fresh" new me...

Judge and Jury

Two flies are buzzing around, one says,
"I see the light", it's so bright, the other
one says, "stay away it's not safe",
but the other does not listen, he flies
towards the light, saying "it's so shiny",
and zap, he's gone.

Two camels' side by side, one says to
the other, "have you got the hump with
me".

Just two simple phrases, but show the
two sides, one shows the obvious
dangers of life, and the constant put me
downs, also only see the good in
everything. The other type, the
persistent, pessimistic, and judgemental
type, who's glass is always half empty.

Once dementia sets upon you, and you
start to decline in health, body and
mind, the world then can-not help itself
in being critical, impatient, and
offensive, and the want to evaluate
everything that's not the "norm".

As a person, a human, you start to see
this world different, at times it shows no
depth, no feelings, or no soul.

It's on those moments that you feel
alone, feel low and distant, but as quick
as you like, it's shining bright, pulling
you through, and on those days, this
world is beautiful, alive, and giving too.

Three or days in a row, I'm sat away,
with my back facing away from this
world, head down, looking but not
seeing, hearing but not listening,
pushing away and a not for wanting
anything.

Then the other days, I'm alive, I'm
going places, I'm seeing faces for that
first time, don't hold me back, I'm
travelling so fast, come along, enjoy my
ride, it will be a "blast".

So, remember we are alive, but
sometimes we have to relax, to sit back
down, to re-adjust, to re-charge, so
we're ready to go again.

I'm sorry now that I have no filter and
it's been snatched away.

Please remember this, then you're see
"I'm not so bad", just different at times.

You are in your car, travelling fast, in
four lanes, with plenty of room and
comfortable too, I'm in my car,
travelling just as fast, but in a single
lane, trying so hard to stay in lane.

These are two examples are how my
brain is now, I'm so hard trying to allow
and push everything through, but yours
is a filter free and goes out with comfort
and ease.

So, STOP, LOOK and LISTEN
and then maybe, you're again that
person I know who's "one of a kind"..

Questions or Answers

Who am I, am I still me, or am I
different even alive?

How did I change, why did I change?

Can I still be me, or have I now left?

What has changed, did I change or did
you?

I'm now fully charged; can you say the
same?
My batteries can get depleted with ease,
but does yours continue to charge, or
does yours also deplete.

Questions, I have many, but the answers
are too few.

Choices are many, they continue to
grow, but are yours still continuing to
grow, or did I stop their growth.

Darkness can cast shadows upon my
path, but you light up my steps, along
its way.

My mind decides to play a game, often does, so can you decide to play along too.

We are as one, in this time and place, we're also one in my "other" place.

Space and time hold no bounds, but sands of time can slip away.

So, hold me tight, hold me strong, and then I'll hold on longer and stronger, with this fight.

I have no answers for you today, you may have many questions, so you can ask away, and maybe, somehow, they're make their way to me, so maybe then, we both can see, what we want to "hear and feel".

Today can be "that" day, but tomorrow can also be better still.so we will make some memories, allowing us
to soldier through, and maybe then, we will see what
"our" future holds...

Stereo Player

Pause, rewind, fast forward or may be
play.

My mind and body are in a constant
"pause", why? I'm still asking myself
this same question.

Is this a way to re-set, to evaluate or to
recharge, not too sure, but it's not good?

Does this pause allow this time of mine
to gain clarity and slow myself down
rather than "pause" my life.

I seem to find the re-wind button, by
mistake, so I constantly ask myself
why? but strangely no answers seem to
be forthcoming.

I have fast amounts of past memories
that have stayed or defined me. These
are ingrained and imprinted, so deep,
that they seem to be in me to the core.

This feels strange, as if I'm in a familiar
re-wind a kind of loop, as I remember
with clarity past memories, but not any
current events.

Has my mind re-winded or re-wound itself to a better safer place to comfort itself, to reassure and allow time to re-align, I'm not too sure why? but if I find the answer, I will share with you.

My days are now on constant "fast-forward", or feels that they are, my mind travels so fast, so confused, not sure why, but definitely not nice.

Everything and everyone seem to be on "fast-forward", they seem to travel so fast, or am I still on "pause", or "re-wind", again not too sure.

My thought process feels the same, but different at times, so am I now the same, or are you all different than me.

I try hard to press "play", I'm not sure why, but I want to play along some more, I'm not ready to "pause, rewind, or even fast-forward", but "play" seems hard to press.

So hard to enjoy or even want.

It's different with me, here on "play",
but please press play, and let's kick start
this mind of mine..

Here or There

I'm here are you there or are you here,
and I'm still there, or are even
anywhere.

As I'm sure, I was here, here
somewhere, I was there but not now.

Whilst I was there I didn't see you, so I
assume you was here.

So then, when I was here, I looked for
you, guess what, you were there.

Surprise surprise I'm still looking for
where you are, I'll keep looking for you
in there, as maybe, just maybe, you will
still be there, in time for me to catch
you there before you are here with the
other me.

I'll keep searching, catching up, as only
then will I be here and there, with all of
you.

So, whilst we are here and now, we're
gather round, we're laugh and cry, as
then when it's time we're all travel there,

as then there will be more to come, for all to share.

So even if I'm in there some more, rather than here and now, I can be alone sometimes, but not alone at all times.

Here in time, I know there will be more of me to bear and to see and if I'm in there too long or too much, please be here, be around, as then when I am here

I'll stick around, as then I won't be there again too long...

Daily Challenges

Today becomes a day, another one,
rotation of time, motivation of my life.

Whether to fight or to sit and relax.

Today can be better than yesterday, but
then again, can it be, maybe it will,
maybe it won't, but I'll see through its
passing as to whether today was better,
or was it just another rotated motion of
time.

Yesterday has gone, let's hope today,
that will become tomorrow, will be a
better one, as I'm hoping it last a little
longer this time, it stays around, it
becomes more intense, to stimulate,
indulge and participate with these
moments of me.

In me today, is here and now, tomorrow
will come and join in with me once
more, and then let's see where I will go.

It may become just another yesterday,
hopefully it will not pass me by, or
leave before it has begun, but instead
last in me that little bit longer.

Tomorrow I'm not too sure about, it
seems to leave some doubts in me, is it
a day for me to forget, or will I even
embrace its approach, another question

I have in me, there's so many, I lose
count, but let's not "start" on that today.
Today can be our day, a day of joy,
memories, and laughter, so I can
explore, continue to grow, so then we
can see what tomorrow will bring.

Days are now in twinned; they just roll
along and definitely merge into one.

I'm not too sure what day it is right
now, so is it today, it could be, or
maybe just goodnight.

I'm all in a daze, as I'm not even sure if
it's night or day.

Forget what day it is, that's not even a
concern now, as I'm all confused with
all these dilemmas, I'm not really
bothered too much now, as I'm sure,
tomorrow will become today for me.
Day after day, time after time for me
now, they are meaningless, they have

no relevance, no concept, or even worth
my acknowledgement.

But I will put one foot forward, one at a
time, to continue to walk with in this
moment.

I will continue to grow, I will need to
rest maybe sometimes, as to regain
momentum and strength, this will allow
more time to be here today, and share
just more moments I'm sharing with
you..

That Special Place

Lie back, relax, close your eyes, clear
your mind, and empty everything.

Allow no thought's, clear all emotions
and negativity, now get ready to open
yourself to all unlimited possibilities
within the realms of "that" special
world.

That place of tranquillity, this place that
is only obtained by these easy steps, but
also can be hard to obtain entry to.
This place allows a natural flow of
balance and time to allow motion and
emotions to re-align and re-charge, it
allows contemplation or reflection of
yourself.

This special place of mind and soul
allows love, comfort, compassion, and
positive thought to nurture and grow,
also develop, and leave in you, all that
you need or wish to keep.

Whilst you are here, in "this" place
allow yourself the pleasures it brings,
open your mind to all its possibilities,

but not it's limitations or it's restrictions,
as these are only set by you.

Your path or journey through into this
place is gifted and should be shared, so
look around, smell the air, and welcome
in all around to what's there for you to
gain.

So maybe then in that moment, you will
share something real and special, and
with that in mind open your heart, your
mind also your eyes and allow it to
flow, allowing it to leave you all in a
glow.

You are now rewarded, you are now
able to share this offering, that's now
your gift, to all special to you.

Once you are ready, and feeling
inclined, you will be ready to open your
eyes and realise, that you are now
refreshed, recharged, and ready to offer
this newfound knowledge of strength, to
cherished one's of those you love,
shower those all around, as then you
will be rewarded in abundance.

Don't forget to look back sometimes and remember where you gained this newfound strength, as it was in this special place, you were given a "gift".

On remembrance with these gifts, from this special place, that now I've shared with you, is where I go to be safe and comforted.

Surprise, surprise, to all of you, this is where I go day to day to stay away, to allow myself some time to switch off, pause and stop.

In this place I'm special, I'm allowed total vision, total value, I'm normal for a while and in my other place, I'm actually me ,the "old" me, fresh out of the bottle, reborn and redeveloped.

Here today I've shared my secret thoughts, I've halved my pain but in this message you will find, that I have gained more than you...

Turn of Events

I went to our local supermarket, just for
a few items, I get myself a small trolley
and enter the store.

I walk down the first aisle, I choose
some flowers for my wife and daughter,
as they needed a boost, a sort of pick
me up.

Then once I walked some more,
"wham-bam" it hit me, no warning, no
trigger, absolutely nothing, all within a
milli-second, I was in another world
and numb far away from where I was.

You would have thought that having a
trolley with the store's logo would have
helped, bringing me back into reality,
but it did not.

I did not know where I was, why I was
there, no explanation of anything, but
surprisingly I did not panic, I was cool
as a cucumber.

There was no trigger point to re-set me,
so I must have thought, I would
continue to walk on, so thing's would

come back to me, but it did not. I was oblivious to the trolley, the flowers, probably 20/30 seconds later I remembered I had something in my pocket, I got it out, it was a short shopping list, but still this did not re-set me.

So, I walked some more, for maybe another 20/30 seconds, then "wham-bam" it hit me, I was back in this world, back to reality.

It was so strange, that feeling of not knowing of who, what, why or even when.

Why did I not grasp the concept of the trolley, the flowers or even the massive supermarket, but no, not me, I was oblivious to all of it.

This terrible disease will show no mercy, no compassion in its growth, it will not discriminate of gender, age, wealth, or health.

It holds no bounds, but only wants to gain in its strength, the hold on you, and its captives, also to do this in a slow,

agonising way, that will not only
destroy your mind, but your soul too.

It will want to digest everything, it will
show no expressions or compassion,
only contempt and satisfaction once it
has it's hold.

This small, short memory of a situation
is only to highlight that we know little,
understand less about this disease, but
yet we will never lose dignity or
integrity with our continued battle to
live life..

The Same but Different

If you can I will, I would and you
should, you lead and I'll follow, in and
out, up, and down, two of a kind, yin-
yang, herbs and spices.
Opposites attract, North and South,
lemon and lime, you and me, sugar, and
spice.

All these seem opposites, the same,
pairs, some way connected, or even an
infinity.

They may even share similarities, but
what comes to mind is, they seem to fit
in the same sentence, a sort of similar
identity.

What I'm trying to say or express is,
that even though we are the same, out of
life's mould, and the same formation,
shaped to fit within a boundary of
acceptance.

But once the mould is either broken or
damaged, then no longer does the
"norm" become able to be made, re-
designed, or created in its "original"
format

The same as all of us, as long as we
keep our shape, fit into the "norm" of
society, follow the guidance set upon
us, and stay within its parameters, then
life and society feels secure, it leaves
you alone, it allows for a natural flow,
and its eyes will not even flicker.

So, the natural balance is set and happy,
allowing the waters to flow calmly.

But then "bang", as soon as you
become, not the "same", not shaped or
designed alike, or fit with what's
acceptable, that's when life and society
allows, ridicule, opinions, and
thoughtless comments.

Because "this" disease is not visual, not
the "norm", it's definitely not obvious
and can hide at will, it makes its
presence at will, it's then when we as
the "chosen" ones, see that not everyone
is, pure, kind, soulful and precious.

Society shows on these time's that,
when the chips are down, only the
"cream" of us will, rise to the challenge
and become either "angels or demons",

become "carers or sharers", or will they become "isolators or dictators".

Do not allow this disease to consume or direct you, but nurture, comfort you, become one with it, make your peace with it, and then maybe it will not become you, or consume us.

As I will not become it, I will not be part of this and definitely not fall in line with it.

I will define myself , of who I am, of who I was and will be, I will define me and my own destination, and I will finish what "it" started.

A disease cannot beat or consume, it may try to win and fight, but it cannot define you, so continue to battle, continue to be you, and never lose your identity, as I'll continue with you..

Focus

My eyes are closed, my head is buzzing,
I'm so tired, but I seem to feel unable to
sleep.

It feels like my eyes are moving trying,
to focus, but not able to see.
The vision seems blurred or blocked by
something.

I'm feeling like I'm at the end of a road,
wanting to cross, wanting to turn right,
or left, but unable to see, how, why, or
even what way to decide to go.

It's as if this decision or choices are not
mine anymore, and it's a strange
sensation.

I hear the buzzing in my head, but at the
same time I don't, it's like I'm having a
headache, but again not. It's like a strain
of some kind.

I have this buzzing most nights, or
before I fall asleep, or should I say, try
to.

Hard as I try, I find focusing forward is
not an option.

I do not seem to find any way forward
of any kind or in any situation.

I can picture previous events and places,
but I don't seem to see anything today
or ahead, it's very strange, and it's not
for the want of trying.

I fall asleep at random, it's like a sport
now to me, I'd probably win a medal if I
was entered.

But when I want to sleep, I'm bloody
wide awake, tired, and frustrated,
staring at the ceiling, thinking, how this
happen to me.

A word banded out there, presented to
the world in a package called
"Dementia".

It seems to be a small, insignificant
word, speak of it to other's and it's "oh
right", and that's because you can't see
it, touch it, or reach for it.

But by "jolly" it bloody well grabs you by both hands, probably while your back was turned, or you were asleep, it's definitely not fussy on who it picks a fight with.

So, I will try to sleep, try to rest, try to relax and whilst I do let's hope I catch up with my body and mind, so I can feel young and energetic again.

I would love to shout, "stop the world I want to get off", but actually on reflection, now at my age, I'd probably just say something like, "wait for me", "I'll catch up", or even "please slow down".

But actually, I'm the one who needs to stop and get off.

So, I'll go and try to sleep, I'll say goodnight and see you soon.

Until we meet again and talk some more, and don't worry if you do not remember, don't fret, I won't too...

Rejection of Deflection

Don't just walk past, don't ignore me,
I'm still me, I know you saw me, as I
did you.

I may from time to time be able to
recognise your face, but that's just a side
issue of what I have, but not an excuse.

But remember I'm here, so please treat
me the same as I treat you, as I'm still
me.

In situations when we feel awkward, we
often show a weakness, but we don't
show our strengths, please treat me as
usual, say "hi" or "How's your day
going", and even if I don't give my
usual happy acknowledgement, just
remember if I could I would and I still
want to be having our friendly banter.

We all have low times or even times
where we want to be left alone, but at
times I do not have that luxury of
choice.

My mind has at times disconnected
itself from me, but I have not

disconnected from you or our loved ones.

I still have the need of normality, similarity, and also a need to be kept grounded.

In that being said, let's not see this change in me as a negative, or an elephant in the room, but a way to challenge our loyalty and compassion in each of us.

So, we make sure we do not fail, but actually it makes us all stronger and wiser.

I try to convince myself that I'm strong, wise, and here to challenge myself during these hard times.

I will not let myself down by being negative, rejective, or selfish.

I will always know within me, I am blessed, loved but at the same time different but most importantly me.

In knowing this I will show
compassion, positivity, emotion, and
love.

I will not show a negative emotion, a
rudeness, or any forms of hate.

Dementia is a just a "word",
It most definitely is not me.
It will never be worth my valuable time
I have left..

Look to the Future

I sat on my recliner chair, pushed it
back and relaxed.

I closed my eyes and faced the window,
the sun was shining through the blinds,
giving of a lovely warmth and glow.

As I began to fall asleep, I felt even
though my eyes were closed, it was
bright, maybe because the sun was so
shiny, or it may have been because I
was so tired, (again), it felt so nice
warm and cosy.

Once I was in a deep sleep, well I knew
I was, because afterwards my wife told
me I was snoring.

I seemed to be blinded by an intense
daze, like it was foggy, it stopped me
from being able to focus.

As I continued to walk, I started to get
through this and got through to a clear
opening, as I did everything became
clearer, more focused, during this
sensation I was walking so relaxed.

Then the grass I was walking on seemed
so white, not a snow look, but
absolutely beautiful. It just felt so
warming, so natural and normal,
at the same time relaxing.

As I carried on walking, it felt fresh,
welcoming, I felt a breeze across my
face, but it was not cold, but a warm
and comforting, it left me feeling
absolutely wonderful.

In the distance I could hear voices, they
seemed to be coming from the hillsides,
as I looked around, I noticed everything
was a warm white colour, a bit like a
scene from a Christmas card, but with a
warm glow feeling.

As I was dreaming, and hearing voices,
I did not feel I was here to see anyone
in specific, a more of just seeing and
looking around.

I felt it was a more of looking in,
through a scene rather than actually me
walking in person, like I was visualising
the time here.

Once I had been here for a while, I felt I had been left with a message, which was, that yes our family and friends are not "waiting" for us to arrive, but actually saying, that they are there for their respite, their paradise and they are living their lives to the max.

They will though be there to "meet and greet" us when, and not for a long time, our time comes.

But they are definitely not waiting, they are having their times of their lives.

So please don't stress or worry about me or them, but live your life, enjoy yourself to the max.

Don't leave the party early but stay for that last dance.

Only then, once you have lived a full and meaningful life, in an honest and loyal way will you be able to say, "I'm ready", then they will be ready to reply, "good to see you".

The warm comforting embrace awaits us all, our time must be spent, learning, listening and live our lives with love to all, then once we have done all these easy steps, our place, our position will be ready and waiting for us, leading us to join our loved ones.

Whether we live long, a short life, or maybe waste it, we all go through the same exit doors, let's just make sure we enjoy our time's, experience it, and embrace life's test put upon us.

Once I enter into my next chapter of life's challenges, I will promise to embrace it, handle it, and show that

Dementia has only captured a part of me, but it will never have my "heart and soul", this is already given freely to my beautiful wife and family.

So sorry Dementia I stick two fingers up at you and say, "up yours".

I will pack my memories and experiences up, store them safely ready for my next instalment, only in this next part will I open this suitcase up at "selected" times, I will cherish them, I may even at times share them with you.

If I do share these moments with you,
please show, compassion and as you do
I will reward you in return, with while I
can, an abundance of love, kindness that
leaves you the richer than you were.

I may not in my future stage express
exactly how much I love you, but
remember at all times you are my rock,
my strength and also my guidance, I am
only half a person without you and my
family....

I am me (sometimes)

Stand up and talk, sit down, and listen,
lie down and wander into.

Whilst I look the same and have good
days, where everything goes well, there
are those darker days too.

I know I may be that person at times,
that darker selfish side of me that pop's
out, but as you see and witness its
appearance, I see how hard I tried to
hold him a prisoner inside of me.

We all try to walk the walk, and talk the
talk, but when "it" hits the fan, only
then will we see loyalty, love, emotion,
and compassion running through their
veins.

I can write at times fairly well when my
mind is doing well, but once that button
switches off, then I cannot even do a
simple task.

This strange situation is just that, a
situation I find myself in, a challenge,
but not one I'm willing just yet to give
up on.

We all find solace, moments and
flashbacks to good times, highlighted
highs from times past.

But we also seem to dwell into gloomy
features, gloomy horizons too often,
without stepping back and re-evaluating
as to what we have, achieved, and
become.

We are stronger than we know, we're
better than we see ourselves and we are
definitely braver for it.

So, as we endure life's challenges, it's in
these negative times that our true
challenges are faced, it's how we assess
and conquer that will define all of us.

No amount of verbal negativity will
help, no put me downs or making
other's feel inadequate will help any
situations.

So, as we stay strong, continue to fight
and conquer, we must show that we are
wiser, stronger and pure, than those
who try to drag us down.

Always remember, you are you, through
and through, but so am I, it's just that
I'm wrapped differently and yes I may
have a few more layers, and yes maybe
wrapped up a bit wonky.

But once the wrappers are off, you're
see me, I am that person who always
put your needs first, I always walked on
the outside, I always opened the door
and definitely always paid.

So yes, I'm still that person, that person
who is loving, caring, sharing, and just
maybe during these dark times I seldom
may appear, but know I am still in
there, just for you, and I'm trying to re-
surface them every waking hour, to
show all of you that you are special to
me.

So, as I pop in and out, as I visit other
places, without ever getting out of my
seat, know if I could show you, that
you're in every trip I make, otherwise it
would be lonely in there.

So, feel happy and content knowing that
whilst I travel, that I'm actually
travelling with all of you, every time.

Feet need to be firm, and know I'm
firmly grounded, as I have a bubble of
security, love, and positivity, I wish this
for everyone who is sadly going
through my journey as well.

I wish you well in your journey, make
sure you enjoy it, stay true to yourself,
don't lose sight of who you are, and
remember in there, deep inside you are
a good person.

I send all my love, thoughts, and
prayers, and until I see you again, keep
your chins up, and a "BIG LOVE" to
you all....

Look, Listen, and then Speak

Look around and what do you see, and
when you do, are you really actually
there, are you focused on what's real, or
just focused on specifics, with the rest is
just a blur.

Do you really see the full picture, or a
virtual reality, just so you can "get by",
to exist within the realms of life's quick
pace?

Then losing sight of what's good around
you, loosing vision of what's staring at
you without you even knowing.

Don't lose focus, stay sharp, be that one
percent who sees everything, listens,
and becomes all the better for it.

Once you start accepting a more
relaxed, slower pace of life, only then
will your clarity be prominent and give
you crystal clear vision of the smaller
things in your life.

Listen do you hear, are you even
bothered to want to know what that
sound was, or was life pushing you

faster, moving you on to your next
destination.

Once you start to really listen, and take
up time to study sounds, movements,
and its beauty, then you will become
more intrigued, more in tuned and more
acceptable to all it's great possibilities.

You may hear sounds for the first time,
even at an older age, as once you put
yourself in a more content relaxed,
stable and steady pace, you will benefit
from those sounds and movements this
wonderful world has to offer.

The beautiful sounds are all around us,
they are free of charge, so grab as much
as you like, as it's a free buffet, and you
can benefit from its abundance, and it
will reward you accordingly.

Speak and you will be heard, speak with
wisdom and the world will hear and
give you an acceptance.

Speak with ignorance and the world
turns away and shows you no mercy.

We all have a voice, we all can be the loudest person in the room, that one person who everyone tries to ignore.

But it's so much better and comforting to be that one person, who can be the quietest.

That one person who captures curiosity, that one person who everyone wants to hear and listen to.

So, before you shout, talk or open your mouth and speak out or up, gather a moment, take a deep breath, pause, think and then maybe you can be that one percent who is so in tuned to a positive and warming embrace to all around.

I am pleased to say, I've been in that one percent, before this stage of life took residency within me.

I was that "go to" person, the one who intrigued those around, showed grace and elegance, showered compassion when needed, I offered comfort, warmth, and opportunities to all, not just selected chosen ones, but all who needed it, but not one's who just wanted it.

On reflection, stand up and enjoy being heard, know when to sit and listen to gain more wisdom in doing so.

Hear what's important, but never to negative, unrealistic visions. Absorb what you need, but not necessarily want, and be more selective in your choices.

Cheapest is not always the best buy.

Hear clearly, talk slowly, listen intensely, offer your hand often, give a warm accepting smile, show compassion as then life and this beautiful world gives back tenfold, but only once you embrace its natural un-tarnished persona.

Hear the birds, smell the flowers, give your life a kick start, and never let anyone make you feel in-adequate, unworthy.

You are strong and good, and once you show courage you become you again.

I will not let my life's challenges beat
me, I'll let them define me, make sure
you do likewise.

Make a promise to yourself, that today
"is my day", put it on repeat, own it and
make it yours.

It's only you who can make that
difference..

When the World Watches on

As time has been passing me by over
the last few months, and whilst I sit and
dwell too much, I seem to of acquired
too many wasteful pieces of
information.

Whilst I sit and contemplate, the world
continues to move on, regardless as to
whether you are in it or not.

It will not wait around for your
permission to stop and definitely will
not slow down for you to catch a ride.

All the time you abide by its rules, you
take up your position within its
structure, its fabrication, then you are
part of its soul, it's wellbeing, you are
part of the cogs that make it turn over
smoothly and quietly.

But once you step off this roller-coaster,
and become detached, you will no
longer be accepted upon its journey or
its destination but set up your own one
alone.

The world will continue to move on regardless, show no emotion and will not look out for your welfare.

But not once would I allow the lack of compassion dissolve my identity, self-belief or my own worth.

I have a resolution within that drives me, it guides me and nurtures my every move.

I have found a new drive in me and "I like it".

It's being grounded, it's like I've had an epiphany, a sort of wake up call.

It's allowed me to see what's real, what is important, it's given me more of an understanding of what and who I am.

Also, what this world takes from us on a daily basis.

All the time you pay, and you contribute, then you are a part of, you are part of the collective.

But once you have to step away from the "norm" you become self-contained, isolated, an individual, not part of the once collective family.

Once the honeymoon period is over, and the shock of realising you are alone, then you will become more resilient, more courageous, and more aware of what actually matters more.

You become more aware of your own morality, also that you are you, and once you find yourself, you can become stronger for it and become the person you wish you could have been all along.

So, whilst others are plodding along, on their "life's" journey, travelling in that one direction, following the path set out for them, following its guidance, you will make sure that you now have an individual choice, an individual decision and voice, so own and express it.

If any part of you shows weakness digest it, turn and guide it away, ignore the ignorance it expels, then move on to the next challenge and adversities.

Convert its negativity into a positivity, grasp it with both hands, then you will become stronger and wiser.

Our challenges are only minor, they will test us, and will allow our faith to be contested, sometimes to the limit, by in it doing so, we hope it set's our own standard for others to admire, to aspire to and leave a memento to this world that we were here.

Allow life only to be a guide, allow others to give an offering, and allow in what's acceptable, but never to digest the negativity.

Allow yourself to grow, allow the wisdom to nurture within. Also allow life to flow through you whilst feeling it's warmth in doing so.

Tell yourself you are worth more than "that", but less than "this", only take what you need not what's wanted.

Allow others to follow you but make sure you follow your own way.

In becoming an individual and
becoming yourself once again, grasp the
concept of being alive, being that so
much more. Once you do, you will be
free to express, to see much more and
with much more clarity.

Challenge your own limitations and do
not accept less than you deserve.
I've left an imprint, I've made a small
insignificant input, it may not be
apparent, but I know it's there, it's
ticking away quite nicely "thank you".

In doing this journal, and where it is
taking me, leaves its own imprint, only
leaves a mark deep enough by its
acceptance from you.

Offer your warm embrace in other
people's defects, their differences and
give your warmth in their coldness.

Share but never smother, sit back, and
observe what becomes of your loving
endeavours towards others.

Make sure your growth is only
restricted by your own abilities, set out
your own clear vision and stay

completely focused never letting others
tempt you away.

This world is your own test, so accept
it, do not always place blame, and
criticise.

Becoming me is the best thing I could
have hoped and wished for, knowing I
have accepted my offerings, I am
breathing better, living wiser and
hearing more.

While you leave love and warmth,
allowing its growth, you will gain from
its returned offering and rewards.

I will leave this journal message open
for your deliverance and whatever it
offers to you.

It is only my opinion not gospel
according to, and please take from it
what you want or need.

I leave you love, comfort, kind wishes,
an open invitation.

Follow your own path, live your life
with love, enjoy all opportunities, never

look back wishing, wondering if or
why.

Strength is within all, individually or
collectively, so share yours around,
don't lock it away...

When Reality Sets In

As days become weeks, that become
months, I have had too much time for
reality to check up on me.

With being diagnosed with vascular
dementia and Alzheimer's back in
March 2021, the Consultant was
understanding, polite and detailed, but
my reality came up and set up home
much later.

I think with all of us, we can feel
invincible, a kind of indestructible
force.

But when something like this hits you,
and with no visible evidence, you
become dismissive in some strange
way.

But once reality starts to creep into you,
it becomes a strange phenomenon, a test
of acceptance and durability.

Even though we all feel like "I'm not
bothered", or "I can handle anything",
reality will inevitably hit home at some
point, and when it does, it's then that

your own strengths and courage will be tested and stretched.

It will be at these times in your life when you either accept and challenge it or fall and have self-pity with the situation.

It can be a time for finding the person within, the person who faces and embraces live, love and happiness. But not accepting the darkness of rejection and negativity.

Families will inevitably want to smother and comfort.

Enjoy it and embrace it, but never patronise this gift, please re-pay it back with a warm comforting arm, that's open wide with your embrace.

Reality is only a perception, a stance of your own acceptance, challenges are and can be daily occurrences, so become stronger with each and every one.

Do not fall at your first difficult test in this life, and if you need, accept the hand of help and guidance, embrace its warmth and kindness, and kick out any wasteful forms of emptiness.

My own reality is here upon me, and with it, I feel stronger for it, a better person for it, and a now a more mindful soul. With it I seemed to of digested its approach, inhaled its challenge upon my body, and I've made the changes within to enjoy each day, or at least the one's I remember.

I will laugh with you, but not at you, I'll accept openness, but I'll reject most definitely sympathy and pity.

My family are and will always be my rock, my stability also my guidance, but then again they always have been, and this has never left me now or before in any doubt.

Make sure you surround yourself in your fight, with family, friends, loved ones, and maybe even distant people.

Enjoy your own company and theirs, wake up each and every day with a smile and a "good morning", as once

you do, the world will smile and love
you more.

I'm a realist, and with this, I understand
what is normal, what is false, what is
now and what actually can be achieved
and understanding realism, I know I can
make choices, well on the "good" days,
I can plan for now, and I can set out
goals within my capacity.

So, in this, it allows me to be me within
a certain degree, allows me an identity,
a self-worth, with an understanding that
I have accepted my changes in my life.

Set out your own challenges, do not
allow anyone to do this for you.

Make sure whatever you achieve and
strive to conquer, know you "did it", not
others.

Know your limits, don't be shying
away, push and challenge them. Keep
your identity and stay true within
yourself.

Look in the mirror, see who's looking
back, is it who you want to see and be.

I know when I look, I see clearly and accept who I am, I know "that" person looking back is not perfect, but in accepting this, know, I'm still trying and striving to be someone, that one percent better and once acknowledging I will see me, and say I'm proud to be me.

Give yourself time to achieve, allow momentum to push you on, stay within your own persona, and make or break your own mould, become that "one of a kind", leave your mark, but keep both feet firmly on the ground at all times. REALITY, is a short insignificant word, but once you have a moment with it, then it's a game changer...

On the Mountain I Gained Me

I walk upon the path of life, and as I do,
I come face to face with something in
my way.

I look up and see the mountain, its size,
its enormous mass.

It's in my way, it's too wide to walk
around, it's too dense to go through.

So, I see no other option, no other
choices, I must face this challenge here
and now.

I will not want to walk back down this
path, as I've been down there, and I'm
not wanting to go back.

This mountain has I feel, challenged
me, a feeling of laughing at me and at
the same time giving a sense of its
stronger and better than me.

So, I will rise this challenge, I will walk
upon its steep sides, and face its
adversities that's been placed upon me.

I make the first steps and as I do, I look
down, I see a beautiful small stone, its
shape, its definition has been designed
by nature itself, over many, many years.

As I placed it in my palm, I saw that, in
that moment, we are we're the same, we
were insignificant, small and shaped by
life itself, so I grasped it tightly and in a
whisper said let's face this challenge
together, it was if this stone had its own
challenge to reach out and reach its goal
too.

I walked, I crawled, and I slipped
several times, I was cut and bruised, I
was damp and cold, but I was not
feeling alone and after much time had
passed I arrived upon its peak, it's
shoulders.
I sat for a while, to gain strength, as I
did I placed this stone upon the peak of
the mountain, as I did I sensed that this
stone had been for so long, looking up
and being stood and stared upon, now it
was above and free to look and gain in
its own sense of achievement.
Only together had we achieved
completion, see upon my arrival here at
the foot of the mountain, I arrived alone

but with this stone in my palm I was not alone.
I took the stone with me at all the times and with this I was never really alone, a reassurance I felt I needed.

This mountain was not here to cast a rejection on me, but to allow me to accept my own challenge, accept my own inability and recognising this, allow me to be who I am and what I can be.

This mountain was all alone, its size and strength were incomparable, it only had itself, was lonely and cold, miserable, in self-isolation, but with me in that moment I was not alone, I was not cold, but more importantly not weak.

In our lives, our challenges can block our paths, we will and can be pushed down, can offer us nothing but try to take everything away.

Take your challenge, face the adversities it brings , break down your own barriers and learn along the road.

Never accept defeat in yourself ,life's
too short and selfish, stand proud up
upon your mountain, take that moment
of satisfaction, but do not stay and gloat
for too long , step away once you
conquer the challenge and move on to
the next one.

Know that in doing so it, cannot change
you completely, but it can allow
movement and growth in your
contention and comfort, allowing you to
push away any destruction or self-pity.

Walk on your path with dignity, head
held high, be proud, accept life will
challenge you, and in accepting all of
this, be true to yourself, at all times
contain your dignity and lock up your
negativity forever, as you do not need it
anymore.

Tests will be placed upon your abilities,
on your path of life, this path will
deviate, lead off and have junctions too,
but stay on your path, make only your
own choices, not those of others around,
listen to yourself, as it's only you who
has the right answer, that's relevant and
exclusive for you.

No one knows you more than you know
yourself, so stay true to yourself,
become that individual person and
allow only your own imagination hold
you back.

All of our path's lead and guide us
differently, they will allow us to walk,
run and sit, but all these paths are set
out the same. Leading us to a final
destination, all paths start and end
equal.

The paths distance is only measured by
the amount you walk upon it, it's you
who can determines its length and its
quality of direction, just remember that
all paths lead back for judgement at its
conclusion.

So do, walk the walk, and talk the talk,
allow its growth to enter you, grow
stronger with others around you, show
that your only weakness in your
strength and offer love and kindness
when there is little on offer.

We all at times will feel alone, will feel
neglected and feel so low, but look

upon these times as your strengths, they will never be your weakness.

When you gain time to reflect upon your journey, make sure it was one of self-learning, one of great achievements and not one that has passed you by.

I leave you with my own kind of understanding, my own form of vision, and my own type limitations, use or disregard them, as they are only those of mine.

But if you wish to read and digest that's fine.

These are not my guides, just a sense of me sharing and giving back something that I thought were worth reading, I'm not here to give any advice, I'm only here to leave a message of positive love and kindness.

On your mountain, stand tall, look up and see what you have achieved, only use it for your own guidelines, not for self-gratification, so do not stay there too long.

Only together do we become more, only with others are we really alive. So don't keep locked away anything, open your eyes wide and see your opportunities appear more clearly.

I can and will accept my own challenges, I can and will accept the offer of your help if it's needed, and whilst in doing so I became more...

Who Are You?

At some point in our lives, we will find
a moment, a slight pause, a reflection
that will either define us or set out a
president in all of us.

I wish that at some point, I will be able
to find that one moment, that I look
upon and feel either it defined me or
allowed me to be who I am now.

Enlightenment is a capability that only a
select few of us can possess or able to
achieve, but that does not distract us all
from trying to strive for or achieve.

All of us have points in our lives, will
determine a direction, that will either
alter or sway our choices, we will need
to focus when these points in life's arise,
and that we make choices that are right
in that moment of our lives.

Judgement will enviably show itself to
all of us at some point on our journey of
life, so let's make a clear vision of
choice, give it every chance to make it
the right one that allows and gives more
than you and I receive.

Make adjustments in yourself, stabilise yourself often, to allow growth and nurture, and as you do, watch the seeds grow, bloom and glow in its glorious splendour and beauty.

At these points in our life, these moments will decide who we are, or will become and hopefully allow the movement and direction in the next stages of our life.

Follow along in the knowledge that we have all been there at some stage, we all have travelled to the same places, but the choices we make here are individual, exclusively and selected by that one person.

In that one moment, please find who you and I are, who you and I want to be one, who we will become.

Only allow a judgement to be the guide, make a decisive choice, stay true to that decision, and allow movement in its outcome.

When you look through the glass, yes
you can look through it, but it's not for
really for just seeing.

So, when you turn the sands of time, the
sand will only allow movement in the
one direction.

These words are only actually
directional, maybe even obvious,
mostly inevitable, but you definitely are
not.

You can have multiple outcomes; you
can have an ability to miss direct or
even deflect at any time.

Only your own limitations can guide
you through to your destination, your
mind will control your reigns, but with
your body you can hold power of
choice, and the freewill become
inevitable.

Grow old and wise, but do not get old
and crumble.

Once you put in more than you subtract,
you will find closure, a notability with
in you.

Your inspirations this can be someone else's aspirations.

Allow all of this to radiate from you and these will be counted and rewarded on your journey through this life.

Continue for you to improve, do not accept anything less of yourself, that others will see or judge as a weakness.

In you, your capabilities, they are limitless, make sure you are capable of being able to be so much more than just another statistic or distant memory.

Your barrier is set only up by you, for you only to break down, so do not allow yourself to stumble and fall, you have set it up, so only you know how to overcome its obstacle.

When you have set out your stall, make an allowance for it to accommodate all kinds of situations, all types of practicalities, and all forms of probabilities.

Once your stall has been set out,
correctly, you are then ready for what
that day will throw at you.

Times, choices, and options can all be
given out by you, but once it's offered it
can be shown in different ways, by
accepting or rejecting them, then that
will at some point define the person you
are at that moment in time.

I will leave you with words, but not
messages, I can give you an offering,
but I will never want to imply, or
implicate and I can accept but not
necessarily want or need any form of
approval.

Love to you all, unconditionally,
without a need for a...
"Return to sender."

A Gift That Keeps Giving

What is a "gift", does it imply an
offering, a warm presentation to
someone, what it can be is a show of a
kindness and a form of generosity too.

Once a gift is given, it can be
immensely satisfying once it has been
accepted.
So, it's a kind of gift that will keep
giving and a kind offering that's infinite.

Those gathered at the moment of an
offering, will feel embraced with its
intention. It can radiate a warm glowing
feeling in its passing of love and
emotion.

So, by offering a gift, or having
accepted one, receive it's thought,
cherish that moment, absorb it's
meaning, and fill yourself with the joy it
has just allowed yourself to be given.

Everyone enjoys gifts at Christmas,
Birthdays and Easter, but the gifts I like
to offer are ones of spontaneous,
unexpected ones and ones that offer the

greatest expression, gratitude, and surprise.

So again, it's a gift that will keep giving, there's never a bad time to offer or present a gift, which will and can offer, compassion and recognition.

It can be offered in love, or a friendship or just in an appreciation, but remember by offering a gift, it will allow a moment to be shared, or give a comfort, but also be given in times of hardship too.

This gift or offering, if given when you took time out of your routine, can offer that someone a sense of sentiment in its deliverance.

Some gifts are often unwrapped , some are invisible or could be maybe unrecognisable, but within its offering, it can give a meaning, a sense, a purpose or even recognition in the person it is intended for, it can give an offering of their immense worth or generosity.

Gifts of love, life, hope, encouragement, and contention are all types of presentations and offerings. These are everyday ones that many people cannot see or choose not to.

But by keep offering them out, without their wrappings, eventually they will be seen, it may be not by the recipient, but may be by others around that one said person.

A gift is not subject to its cost, a price tag, it cannot be measured by its size, or by its weight. But it can be judged by the way it is offered, or the thought behind the sentiment it was intended and the context of its meaning.

We all love to receive a gift and that's obvious and fine, some love to give more than they receive. But only a few of us will offer, present, and move on, without the want for a recognition, and it's these types who go around unrecognised and allow us all to go about all the better for their kindness.

I do strive to be one of those kind of person's too, the ones who constantly

will offer, ones who give by far more
than they receive and one whose drive
is to be that one better individual person
and not one of the collective
collaboration that will become lost
within the group.

My gift is of one I will want to offer
always, one that can be shared,
embraced, and left unwrapped, it's not
the one that's needed, but it can be
generously accepted.

It can be just a simple act of kindness,
or a gift that will keep giving, it may
even be one that cannot be ever
measured or contained, maybe not even
held by just that one who's alone.

I want my offerings to be constantly
allowed to be shared, so to allow it
intension be seen, and to be embraced,
accepted by all my loved ones.

Step Up or Step Down

I do not see the need in me to have to step down from this test life has placed upon me.

I will and want to step up and play the long game, that I know I have within me.

I have stepped up on numerous times, over many years to face my adversities and in these moments I have come through that much stronger and feel more complete for it.

To have to step down, I could not accept, as it could or would show negativity, but if I am stepping down, have I? or have I stepped aside, to judge the situation, so I can allow myself to actually step up and made the correct choice, that benefited not just me, but those around.

I shall and will step up when it is needed in me, especially when called upon by my family, even if I cannot stand up or step, up as my resilience will allow for me to be counted for.

Steps of life are always directional, they are our guidelines, to allow us to travel wisely, correct and in the right direction.

They can allow us to improve our position or gain the advantage, but they can also lower ourselves at a time of needs and must.

Choosing to step up, down or away, will or could give a direction to its benefactor once it has been accepted.

But once you have stepped away you have made a decisive move, a choice and only you then can alter its final destination and outcome.

Once you have decided to step down, you have chosen a small change in the direction in your own perception in life.

But step up, then that implies that you have made a directional decision, it's one to be taken lightly, easily, or quickly.

But as you stand up and be decisive,
you will implicate your intension of
stability and given a guidance.

Give witness, that in every step you or I
make, we are constantly becoming
increasingly one directional, as all paths
lead to the same exit.

In the steps we choose will allow others
a perception of us and who we are.

So, what really is a step, is it even a
thing, is it real, or just there all around
us, is it in everything we do, in what we
achieve, or what we imply.

Remember each and every step we
make, are only guides, directions,
allowing us a movement in what we
have, what we are and what can be.

Step by step, we all will move to
another destination that has already
been or accepted as predetermined or
allocated and been set out for us.

So, whether at times, you or I continue
to step forward or backwards, or to the
side, its direction is only really one

way, leading you and I along this path
that's been gifted, even before you and I
were born.

This path can shelter you, can safeguard
your faith, it can allow a guidance of
love, it can bring its rewards in
abundance, but it can only gently guide,
as all our final destinations are or
should be predetermined.

Make allowances, allow yourself
alternations, even allow simple
imperfections occur, but make your
steps be really unique, different from
those have trodden here before.

In your own unique design, there is
character, there is an ability, that is
creative and an emerging imagination,
so allow only you to decide the
complete image that is worthy of your
total contention and satisfaction.

Once you captured your own mind,
reach out and touch the stars, knowing
that you have allowed yourself to be
who you want to be with total peace and
harmony.

Steps can be whatever you want them to be, they can be helpful, or can be annoying, they can be an offer or a removal of your choice. It's the acceptance of them that gives purpose, practically and your improvement.

Are you all ready to step up or down, have you even considered the opportunity it can offer or is there no way you can accept your choice or choices?

I individually have made my steps, I have stood firm, tall, and stood accountable of my own decisions.

Only I can be me, it's only me who can be allowed to cast, only I who can set my own footprint...

Accountable for

There are more stars in our multi-universes than there are grains of sands on our planet.

We know more about the surface of the moon, than we do about our oceans. We only have 1% knowledge of our seas, but yet we are obsessed with travelling to far distant planets, for what purpose or even why??

Every day creatures become extinct, even before our knowledge of their existence.

Our world is a wonderful, beautiful gift, that needs to be cherished, nurtured, protected, and invested into.

This great world, gifted to us, is only on loan, God allows us to occupy it, "rent free", allowing us to be, it's guardians, it's protector and we need to understand the practicalities of that commitment.

Morals, choices and standards are set out or placed out, to allow us to set an example, a standard we require, and we can set our own qualities or our own equalities.

We can show our concerns, but rather than containing them, we can share with others, we can share the opinions, we can express and insure we govern our own directions of intent.

See we seem to allow the flow to be guided for us, only allowing it to flow in one way, but if you sail across the waters in your own direction, you can be that one individual soul, that sets the standard, that allows others to be guided by and with this allowing future choices of a cleaner, better, and protective environment that benefits all.

Individual people can make very small alterations and movements in others, we can make the wheels of motion turn, in doing so allow a larger perception to unfold.

So, in reality, we can all make sacrifices, we can all change what is wrong, to a what is right, even by making slight alterations each and every day.

Allow correct, decisive and positives guide your thought process in its direction of choice, allow yourself the rewards to capsulate you.

You can be a wonderful, powerful, colourful inspiration to others.

Our world needs creative, imaginative, and courageous people to educate and invest knowledge in others, to make wise choices in their future endeavours.

In knowing what our beautiful world has to offer in its beauty, and the creatures around us who rely on us for their protection, can offer us potential and great responsibility.

Can this responsibility offer us new challenges and awareness of what's needed and deserved, I say definitely yes?

But we can all take this responsibility and run with it, we'll that's the ultimate question that only you and I have the answer to.

Allow your heart and soul be your
guide, allow wisdom to control your
choices and know what's acceptable in
your own offerings.

Nurture or nature, whatever, only you
will define the next step of the
evolution, it's our choices that govern
our worlds existence and sustainability.

Greatness can fall upon even the most
insignificant individuals, but standing
up being accountable, we'll that's what
will define all of us, in a moment of a
decisive deliverance.

Our minds are our powerful engines,
our minds can allow great advances if
it's worth advancing towards.

In how we move forward,
in how we accept changes, in how we
can improve within, can be actually our
next great invention.

In all of us we can accept a change, we
easily can adapt, and we all can have
abilities that allow us to want to strive.

So, as we change, whether it's through our minds, our bodies, our culture's, believes or even perception, we need to be in control, keep focused on what's important to others, not just ourselves.

Our circumstances change, they can or will alter frequently, but accepting change can return more than you or I will know. They can offer a start, or end to a segment of our lives.

Our world is ours to enjoy, our lives to be lived, our minds to be explored, and to see what our world is offering us. But remember to replace more than you take away.

In knowing what has been achieved, that has been explored, taken away, been wasted, and extinguished will lead to a greater knowledge.

Wisdom, positivity, and correction can be our inspirations and should not be our aspirations. These can allow opportunities in our improvements and development.

Let you and I become more than what's been before, let's be more than others have left behind for us to correct and allow our future generations marvel in our endeavours.

Never Stand Alone

What if you or I had a sense of having
no love, no emotion, no desires, and no
commitment.

We had no will, no affection, and no
possibilities.

We both then would have a sense of self
sufficiency, a self-sustainability, and no
need of others.

Would it allow or represent that
evolution has allowed us both to be a
more improved version of others, that
have been before, so we could become a
more practical, superior model.

Or maybe a more realism is, that we are
all dependant on someone or something.
That we cannot see, or maybe choose
not to accept, or understand, that we are
all dependent on, rather than isolated
alone.

Place a grain of salt in the palm of your
hand, observe it's structure, it's
compound and you will see its density,
it's strength, and as you do, understand

that we are just a small particle , one of
an individual soul that exist and is
vulnerable, but within our own
structure, we can perform better and
stronger together, allowing growth in
our own progression and motion, so in
our scope to be so much more.

See with, rather than alone, you and I
are the same, we are accepting of our
family, a group that allows harmony, a
peace and tranquillity to blossom in
both of us.

We should not become complacent in
our own self-gratification, or in our own
perception, but we could be rewarded in
multiples, if we accept being part of,
and allowing comfort from this.

Being alone has I'm sure, a sense of
one's own invincibility, one's own
contempt and a sense of me against
them.

But in allowing your mind, body, and
soul, to hear and understand properly,
shows you have visualised its rewards
of being part of something , and you

have not accepted isolation or even a desperation.

In your deliverance into the group and it's embrace, will give you a personal sense of glory and power.

When chosen to be alone, we will have had a time to develop doubts and miss-guided emotions, allowing the time to aim harm without merit or content towards others.

By offering an acceptance of the collective, you've shown an understanding of who and what you are, you have allowed positivity and construction be more of a, rather than a destructive of.

You and I can accept a need for isolation from time to time and that's fine, as it's a selective judgement, it's for a need to step back, and for a reflection of a, rather than, a what if.

But staying alone and isolated by one's own choices, without purpose, and without provocation, will only reflect desolation, unwise or an uncomfortable perception , as nothing of being alone can ever really offer any form of quality or self-improvement.

Within every aspect of our lives, nothing can be completed alone, it cannot be a realistic option, it can only be a perception of an idea, but it is actually only an illusion of your own imagination.

A single soul can never be really totally alone, it's having to be dependent at some point on, food and water, or shelter from the world's offering, and you will daily hold your hand out and accept its deliverance to you.

Our soul continues to improve our knowledge, it's understanding of our desires and these partner our memories well after our bodies have departed from this beautiful earth.

We take our genetics, our continuous commitment to our new environment, that will shed us of, useless, obsolete, and impractical formalities, that are no longer required or needed.

We arrive there refreshed, re-invented and reborn, to be part of a loving, beautiful large family once again, and in this acceptance, we will see that the journey was never taken alone, it was taken collectively, and it arrived in its destination with abundance.

Final chapters in any diary any journal, or of any life experiences, will offer an insight into that one person. It will allow a perception of who that person was or is.

But what is a final chapter, is it really a signing off, to say this is it for now, or this has now finally come to a conclusion and found its natural ending.

But remember, nothing is ever really final, no chapter really ever ends, everything eventually gently fades away, and become detached, they become a memory, but they cannot really be completely forgotten.

A final chapter leaves a question and an answer in itself, as to, is it really. ???.

So, I will sign off, I will not imply that it's my final of anything. I will just allow my words to cease flowing, to allow you to write down your own words, that will allow the continuation into a new chapter and that will allow a journey that I hope never ever concludes.

Love, hope, joy, happiness, and peace will and shall continue to be enjoyed and embraced long into the distant future, so leave loads of happy memories, give out continuous hope, embrace the joy of your beautiful family and allow peace and happiness flow eternally..

Who me???

I wake up 4am, but I'm still tired??

I go to bed at 8pm, as I'm still tired???

I cat nap throughout the day, as I'm still tired???

I say hardly any words all day, but talk all night in my sleep, so is that why I'm still tired???

I only move from chair to toilet, to kettle back to the chair, is that why I'm still tired???

If I get taken out, which is occasionally, I arrive home and surprise, that's why I'm tired???

Am I finding today, whilst I'm on this planet, able to see a pattern emerging, or am I on just repeat???

In my head I'm alert, I'm busy, I'm practical, I'm helpful and yes capable, but in the eyes of another, I'm dazed, I'm accountable, I'm annoying, I'm a burden and probably a miserable so and so, it there another pattern emerging???

Am I today a realist, tomorrow will I be an optimist, or maybe next time a pessimist???

I will emerge from time to time, out of this cocoon of mist, to offer glimpses of my old self, to offer that wisdom I once had, even though you now, may know more than me???

Enlightened moments of genius can pop out randomly, ideas could surface spontaneously without warning, but confusion will probably announce itself frequently, is this all too much to grasp or to contemplate???

On these special days allow your beautiful hand to reassure me, allow your smile to radiate into my direction, gladly offer your assurances that you are still my one true guardian angel, especially in this mad, fast, and obsessive world, so can you please do that for me???

If I appear confused, if I appear dazed,
if I appear not quite me, allow your
brilliance to nurture and ground me, that
will lead me back into the arms of my
loved ones, again, can you also do that
for me??

See as you now are aware, I need you
more than you need me, I offered love,
warmth, comfort, and undying
unconditional love when I was me, now
all I ask for is consideration, guidance,
and assurances, is that possible???

Little by little, day by day we are
cemented by our nobilities, our sense of
morals and our own containment that
can reach far beyond our imaginations...

Is it a word or an excuse?

Dementia, I have it, so do many others.

Does it discriminate, does it select by
age, colour, or wealth, or by something
unseen or unexplained.

The word itself seems to imply that
you're not quite right, something
twisted, the word seems so final and
harsh, DEMENTIA.

Once that figuratively speaking, the
bandages have come off and time has
set in, reality cements itself, it's then
excuses, or wrong decisions come into
play.

We offer, we can imply, and we all can
and do make allowances, or even
accommodate this new unfounded
situation. But over the next levels or
stages, the novelty and sympathy will
have worn /eroded away to a very thin
layer.

The strain can expose the frailties, the
emotions can become stretched, and the
patience becomes literally just bearable.

Our intensions become weighted, or
that our offerings can become a curse
and our futurist ambitions are withered
away.

DEMENTIA, this word seems more
really harmful or painfully hurtful as
time pushes our journey on.

As we travel through this, we can
become individually restrained within
this enforced directive challenge.

I had set my goals for a journey that did
not include this unwanted detour, but I
do not wish for your eternal journey to
be governed by my illness or default.

So, if these unwanted, or unwarranted
pressures unease or have contained your
personal ambitions, then please do not
stop living or form restraints I have put
upon you, please go and free yourself,
with no guilt or judgement placed upon
you, as I do not strive to allow this
unfair pressure to continue unjustly.

See, a compassion is an allotted
allowance, that needs to be allowed to

be grown, by restraints there can be no
compassion only contention.

I would rather this awful disease finish
its harmful damage on me, sooner rather
than later, I would gladly offer it the
whole of me, rather than allow it to chip
away of what's beautiful in my life now.

Choices can be made and accepted by
both inviting parties, but once one of
the recipients is unwell or incomplete,
then those choices are not as intentional
or as grounded in their intended content.

If my inabilities are obvious to
witnessed, then can I really be judged
with such awful feelings, is it
acceptable to be punished with every
negative action possible and in the
verbal contents thrown in my direction
continually.

DEMENTIA has within me a growth, it
has a foot hold, that continues to erode
away. It's on a slow continuous
infectious and viral downward
spiralling negative direction.

I did not wish, want, or ask for this, so
please allow that to reflect within your
future decision making, or in the wise
judgements you may decide to make.

I can now only offer part parcel of a
delivery that wanted to be so much
bigger and better than now is or should
be.

I offer more than a now can deliver, less
than you really deserve, I wish to never
take, but only to receive what's being
delivered in kindness.

I wish for a redemption of what's to
come next, but also a glimmer of hope
that the suffering is short in its offering,
that does not erode that what, once what
was so magical.

Printed in Great Britain
by Amazon

39156721R00086